# THE CRY OF OUR CHILDREN

## Inspirational Journey to Self-Discovery

# RUTH ANDREWS GARNES

*Library of Congress Control Number: 2025906456*

ISBN
978-1-964488-69-1 (Paperback)
978-1-964488-70-7 (eBook)
978-1-964488-68-4 (Hardcover)

"The Cry of Our Children" highlights social issues. It gives tribute to some who lost their life in tragic circumstances and is to inspire hope in those left behind.

*The way we love affects every aspect of life starting with our personal relationship and that effect trickles down into our community and beyond.*

Dr. Kings said, "We are all tied together in a garment of mutual destiny."

With all the advancement, we still struggle with social and political issues but love brings people together. It is important to know that all our actions have cause and effect even the way we love.

This gripping edition of the book delves deep into the pivotal events that have shaped me. It unveils the forces that compelled me to pen the words within these pages. For me, creative writing isn't just a pastime; it's a lifeline, a way to cope rather than a cry of rebellion or a signal of animosity toward others. My experiences have fueled an unquenchable desire for a world free of discrimination. This edition also features song lyrics from my published work, **Songs by Ruth**.

# TABLE OF CONTENTS

PREFACE ................................................................. xiii

Validation and Empowerment ............................................ xiv

Validation and Trust ........................................................ xvi

Left Alone to Fight .......................................................... xviii

Disregard and Neglect ...................................................... xx

Resilience ...................................................................... xxii

Perseverance ................................................................. xxv

Healthy Boundaries ......................................................... xxvi

Reflection ...................................................................... xxvii

## FROM CHILDHOOD CERTAINTY TO ADULT-ANXIETY

Personal Significance ........................................................ 1

Envision Change! ............................................................. 2

Dr. King's Dream ............................................................. 3

Fight! ............................................................................. 5

Every Parent's Dream ....................................................... 6

Walk to the US ................................................................ 7

World Without Border .......................................................... 8

Bring down the curtain of indifference. ................................. 9

Home ................................................................................ 10

Constant haggle .............................................................. 11

Born To Live A Lie .......................................................... 12

Good Girls, ...................................................................... 13

Uncertainty ...................................................................... 14

Indifference ..................................................................... 15

Brother: I get your seething anger. .................................. 16

Boomerang! ..................................................................... 18

Foundation of Peace ....................................................... 19

To always be, .................................................................. 20

Mother ............................................................................ 21

The Cry of our Children ................................................... 22

Hatred ............................................................................. 23

Love should be embraced. ............................................... 24

No Comfort or Reward ..................................................... 25

I Need to go to rehab ...................................................... 26

Blinded by grief, ............................................................. 27

All is Well ........................................................................ 28

Victory Worth Knowing. 29

Survivors win 30

Red, White and Blue that you defend 31

King Solomon's Beauty 32

Boodilicious Lady 33

Heaven Must Have Sent You. 34

Lamborghini 35

Love Song 36

Foot Prints in the Sand 37

Unstoppable 38

It's not personal. 39

The Brave 40

True Hero 41

Passion's Power 42

I'm Living My dreams! 43

September 44

I Use What I have 45

Burning Bridges 46

Cuts Me In Two 47

A Place of Love 49

Things We Need to Discuss .................................. 50

Tight fitted Jeans ........................................ 51

If Only ................................................. 52

I can see clearly that, ................................... 53

A Question for Love. ..................................... 54

A Message for Love ...................................... 55

Story Book Of Love ..................................... 56

The Thoughtful Spouse, .................................. 57

Words Alone ........................................... 58

It's A Woman's Thing .................................... 59

Man of My Dreams ...................................... 60

Smoky Mirrors ......................................... 61

A Million Times ........................................ 62

Love's Secret .......................................... 63

Love isn't Giving in .................................... 64

Not Going to Break Me! ................................. 65

To Put Me Back Together ................................ 66

The Heart Reveals a lot about a person, .................. 67

Rhythm and Blues ...................................... 68

Puzzle Pieces .......................................... 69

Undone ............................................................ 70

Men vs Boys ..................................................... 71

Stand Up to Abuse ........................................... 72

Loved My body: ................................................. 73

Strong but Fragile ............................................. 74

At the Edge of Water, ...................................... 75

Strength as Seen in Women, ............................ 76

Woman in the Mirror, ....................................... 77

Mutual Love ..................................................... 78

Crush ............................................................... 79

Love I Desired .................................................. 80

Only One Dances ............................................. 81

Lover of My Soul .............................................. 82

You, More than Anyone .................................... 83

Happy Monday .................................................. 84

Self-Expression! ............................................... 85

Better! .............................................................. 86

Go away ........................................................... 87

Broken people can be repaired. ........................ 88

How Could I choose someone who rejected me? ... 89

My Thoughts, My Savior ................................................. 90

Playing in the Rain ..................................................... 91

Artist's Aim ............................................................ 92

I Choose Life ........................................................... 93

Live, Love and Learn .................................................... 94

Good Things Given ....................................................... 95

Misguided, ............................................................... 96

Learned Response ........................................................ 97

Be My Example ........................................................... 98

Quality Investment ...................................................... 99

My Actions .............................................................. 100

History ................................................................. 101

Paper-Mache' ............................................................ 102

Persistence ............................................................. 103

Vices and Virtue ........................................................ 104

Created Hell ............................................................ 105

Unexplainable! .......................................................... 106

Gone! ................................................................... 107

Living with Angels ...................................................... 108

Show me how to Grow ..................................................... 109

South Bound ............................................... 110

Finally, Happy ............................................ 111

Color me! Make me brand new. ............................. 112

Life's no game ........................................... 113

Value! ................................................... 114

Replicated Differences ................................... 115

Out Cry! ................................................. 116

Healing Touch ............................................ 117

Courage in Illness ....................................... 118

Trading Places ........................................... 119

I Wear My Wounds as Badges. .............................. 120

This Kind Of Love ........................................ 121

The love I want is the love I give. ...................... 122

Not For my Ear only ...................................... 123

Rain ..................................................... 124

Mirror, Mirror, you think you know me, ................... 125

Calculated Risk!   · ..................................... 126

Quiet Day ................................................ 127

From My Window, I've been watching. ...................... 128

In God, We Trust ......................................... 129

Tribute to America and Paris .................................................. 130

Simply Beautiful ................................................................... 131

Tweet from God .................................................................... 132

God Listens ......................................................................... 133

To Love and Be Loved ........................................................... 134

My Summation ...................................................................... 135

To Live as I Imagined. ........................................................... 136

In The Arms of God ............................................................... 137

Song of Thanksgiving. ............................................................ 138

Sweet Spot ......................................................................... 139

The Final Appeal .................................................................. 140

# THANK YOU FOR READING MY BOOK

# PREFACE

In the wake of recent tragedies, I questioned whether the cries of our children are heard.

Simultaneously, in the middle of life I battled issues I could never accept, *it transformed me*, opened my eyes and changed my beliefs. While I was mainly saddened, I became determined to put a new collection together. I knew that the legacy I wanted to leave would be of my poetry writings, not the issues that I faced. I rise, fall and triumph by my desires and determination, not illness, being left behind, unpublished or forgotten.

As a writer and poet, my *purpose is to bring awareness, then hope and eventually change.*

I wrote this collection at one of the lowest points of my life as I struggled with medical and marital issues.

I grew up in a very dysfunctional home and because of the wounds from my past I needed a lot of affirmation and love. I found that genuine love and care was extremely scarce. However, through my experiences, I became even more convinced that love and not being vindictive or authoritative is the key to healing the past.

I was about seven years old, my older brother Gilbert was eight, and we were accompanied by our four-year-old brother Paul and two-year-old brother Mark. We were entrusted with the task of watering our grandfather's horse—an important duty because this horse was his main mode of transportation. Our maternal grandparents resided in rural Belize, living on acreage across from an empty plot of land that used to be a sawmill. That property had large mounds of sawmill dust and a pond at the rear.

We had done our daunting task many times before, so we had no reason to fear. School-aged children like us believed we could water the horse safely and return home without incident. The hidden danger on that property, an old well, was something we had managed to avoid many times. So, there was no need to worry as we set out, leading the giant beast by a rope attached to his bridle.

Gilbert took the lead, and with obedient clippity-clappity steps, the horse followed us. The journey to the other side went smoothly, as it always had. Our favorite pet hung his head, consuming gallons of water, while we waited patiently. Suddenly, I realized our two-year-old brother Mark was no longer beside us.

Panicked, I exclaimed, "Gilbert, Mark is gone!" Gilbert quickly assessed the situation and told Paul to hold the reins. He then deduced that Mark must have fallen into the old well.

In the rural areas of Belize back in the sixties and seventies, wells were dug as a source for water, even though a fresh water pond was only a few feet away. This well had a ledge four to six feet down before it plunged into darkness. Gilbert and I knew where the gaping hole was, but we had not thought to guide the younger ones away from it. Mark had taken that fatal step and plunged into the hole, landing on the ledge.

Looking down into the hole, we saw Mark still standing on the ledge.

I asked Gilbert if I should go get Granny, but he responded, "No, we don't have time for that." He quickly laid on the ground and instructed me to hold his feet.

"When I say pull, you pull," he said. At seven years old, I had to muster all the strength I could to pull both my brothers up out of that hole.

I held on as tight as I could and lowered Gilbert into the hole until his hand reached Mark's. "Pull!" he commanded. With all the strength I didn't know I had, I pulled my brothers to safety. We got Mark up, and Gilbert took the rope from Paul. We headed back across the road and told our grandmother what had happened. She seemed unbothered, but the most mind-boggling part of this occurrence was two days away.

Our parents were in New York at the time of the incident. A few days later, we received a letter from our mom. In it, she asked her mother not to let the baby go on the old sawmill grounds because he was going to fall in the well. No one outside our household knew that Mark had fallen in the well. Reading my mother's words, my grandmother was completely shocked. My mother wrote that she had dreamed Mark fell into the old well on the property where the sawmill was. In those days, there were no telephones in the village, and important messages were delivered by horseback. Letters between the United States and Belize took one to two weeks to arrive.

One startling thing about my grandmother was how unbothered she used to be, a virtue I admired. She had a serene way of handling situations, unlike my dad, who was high drama. This difference in approaches affected how I dealt with future challenges. As I grew older, I spent less time with my grandparents and more time with my father. That experience significantly impacted my current disposition, making me frantic and anxious if no one acted on the information I provided about impending events. The lack of response heightened my anxiety, creating a persistent sense of urgency. This anxiety contrasted sharply with the calm demeanor of my maternal relatives.

Despite some challenges, the days of living with my grandmother were happy times. My grandmother took great care of us and intervened to address bullying we faced. After dealing with those issues, we had no more mishaps, and the breeze from the pine ridge where she lived was glorious. I still recall the white sandy texture of the property and the green grass and other native plants filled our surroundings with nature's fragrance.

One day, as I sat on the stairs enjoying the beautiful surroundings, I had a vision. My grandmother's mother, Emily, who was 97 years old, came to me. I went to my grandparents and told them about it.

My grandmother, addressing my grandfather, said, "This means she is traveling." That was her way of saying Emily was dying. My grandfather set out to fetch a relative to stay with us as my grandmother prepared to go to her mom. Shortly after my grandmother left for her mother's house, a nephew arrived on horseback, looking for her. I informed him she had already departed.

Throughout my life, whenever I shared my visions, my mother never doubted me, just as her mother had trusted my insights. However, as an adult, I have become guarded about revealing certain aspects of myself due to how individuals have responded to me. My medical claims were once regarded as delusions, conditioning me to hold back and not volunteer certain information. This is a stark contrast to my childhood, when my revelations were believed and acted upon.

During the year I lived with my grandmother, the Catholic school we attended didn't have a uniform policy, so students dressed according to what their families could afford. Our parents were in the United States, and our clothing, purchased from there, stood out. Unfortunately, this made us targets for bullying. One day after school, a bully was pushing my brother around. As he hit my brother, I rushed in to defend him. My younger sister ran away to avoid the fight. Seeing Sharon running away, my brother left me to face the bully alone while he ran after her. The older, bigger boy mercilessly punched me in the stomach, cheered on by the other children. The wind was knocked out of me. I entered the fight to assist my brother but was left to fight alone.

As a grown woman, the scenario of being left alone to fight was far more brutal than my first experience, and the effects of my adult experience were much more debilitating. Folks I was convinced would have stood with me bailed. A few faithful friends remained and were there for me as I endured many trials and tribulations.

All this came at a time when I was on Raloxifene, a medication I was supposed to take for five years following breast surgery and a biopsy that produced a diagnosis of lobular carcinoma in situ. This medication caused drowsiness, and I mostly felt out of sorts. In addition to Raloxifene, I was on other medications that worsened my anxiety and neurological symptoms. Despite seeing a neurologist, my struggles continued for two years before these issues were resolved. They performed an MRI after my initial complaint and claimed it was normal. Yet I continued to feel increasingly unwell. With that, I kept returning to the doctor, begging them to repeat the MRI.

While I received excellent support for my breast care, my neurological care was starkly different. The doctors I saw were confident in their abilities to interpret tests and completely disregarded my symptoms. Claiming I had migraines without an aura, they loaded me up with medication that made it even more difficult for me to manage daily activities. When I tried to explain that the treatment was making things worse, the neurologist dismissed my complaints, insisting my symptoms were unreal and that I needed neuro-psychological testing.

Once again, I became that seven-year-old girl entrusted with this weighty load, leading her horse to the pond but finding it wouldn't drink. This time, I appeared surrounded and supported but was taking on all the blows alone. Burdened with symptoms and conflicted because I was once a registered nurse and felt certain that my dizziness and problems with verbal expression were due to brain issues. The radiologist and the doctors who reviewed my MRI all agreed that the MRI was completely normal. Who would take me seriously? Everyone was convinced that my complaints were unfounded. In my childhood, the woman in charge of my welfare trusted me completely. As an adult living in the United States, I was surrounded by professionals whose sound judgment was essential for me to maintain a relatively normal and healthy life. However, seeds of doubt were being planted, invalidating my reality.

As a former registered nurse, I was confident in my understanding of what was necessary to obtain a diagnosis. I agreed to undergo the neuro-psychological test on the condition that I would also receive a repeat MRI with contrast. Although this repeat test had been previously ordered, insurance refused to cover it, citing that the initial MRI was normal.

I was convinced that I had brain tumors, but the medical gaslighting was causing me severe anxiety. The lengthy diagnostic process and being told that my symptoms were not real took a toll on my mental health. When they asked if I ever saw or heard things, I dared not mention that I occasionally had visions of future events, fearing I would be labeled as schizophrenic. Without scientific data to support such capabilities, they would likely have added more dysfunctional labels. I kept that information hidden, fearing further medical misdiagnosis.

*The only rationale that justified this negligence and harsh mistreatment, I was convinced, was because I was a woman of color.*

During this era, the media was saturated with reports of the unjust killings of minorities. This reinforced my belief that the mistreatment I experienced was an abuse of power. My already burdened mind felt even more targeted when I saw Christian posting support for the killing of George Floyd on social media over a fake twenty-dollar bill.

After I shared my struggles of getting a diagnosis with someone online, a woman responded, "for Pete sake go find yourself a Black doctor!"

Reflecting on those harsh words, I thought about how, as a nurse, I always treated everyone with dignity and respect, regardless of skin color or race. In moments like those, I turned to my pen to unburden myself. Through poetry, I carved out cures for human woes, writing words of support for the unsupported and unloved. I began this collection in 2015 and continued writing until 2017, when I was finally diagnosed with two brain tumors.

After receiving brain surgery and gamma radiation, I developed nerve damage. I didn't want to return to the doctor who dismissed my issues as mental. I chose a white male doctor in her stead who practiced out of the same office. That ended up being another horrible experience as he chased me out of the patient area without examining me. When I reported all these happenings to the Texas medical board, they responded that it was the physician's choice to treat or not to treat a patient. I questioned the humanity in this and where did the oath to do no harm factor in all this. I had genuine medical issues, not just emotional ones. It felt like I was being kicked when I was at my lowest.

As a child, my grandmother was my advocate, but as a hurting adult, the fight was mine alone.

In my pre-teen years, my spirit was crushed, not by discrimination, but by deeply disheartening events. As a person of authority crushed my already fragile ego, my feelings of despondency started to take shape from this tender age. Here I found myself facing issues that would determine the quality of education I received and my tendency to give grace to others who had stepped all over me.

At age twelve, I contracted hepatitis A at a critical time in my life. I was on the verge of taking pivotal exams that could earn me a scholarship to high school. In Belize, scholarships were awarded to the top one hundred students nationwide, and high school education came at a significant cost. My dream was to be among those top performers and attend the best school.

However, hepatitis forced me to stay home for months, causing me to fall behind in my studies. I knew my parents couldn't afford the school I longed to attend, so I had to excel. My dedicated teacher volunteered to tutor me at home, wanting me to succeed. The severity of the illness held me down, making it hard for me to concentrate.

I vividly remember my dad sitting a few feet away, observing as my teacher tried to help me grasp the lessons. It became clear that my illness was too severe that I could not follow along nor keep up with my studies. It was decided that I would pause my education until I fully recovered. At the time, I was too sick to feel disappointed, but the weight of that disappointment hit me hard later on.

I was part of a close-knit class; we had been together since kindergarten—except for the year I spent with my grandparents in rural Belize in a village called Bermudan Landing. Upon my return to Belize City, our bond remained unbroken until my recent absence due to illness. I believe my classmates were silently worried about me, though some explanation was given to the class.

On my first day back to class, the classmate who sat next to me was eager to catch up and talk. Feeling the pressure to catch up on my studies, I asked her to be quiet. She ignored my request and continued talking. After asking her two more times, frustration boiled over. I raised my voice and, with harsher tones, told her to shut up.

The teacher, hearing my outburst but not considering that this was my first day back, told me to stand outside in the scorching sun. This had gone beyond a simple exchange between my classmate and me. It was my response that caused her to react more harshly. The teachers was the exact person who offered to tutor me at home, and visibly saw my struggles, but in this moment, that caring side of her was gone. As I told my classmate to shut up, the teacher lifted her head from her reading and defended my classmate.

Her exact words were, "You little Bermudan Landing monkey, you're as miserable as your Grandma Hulse."

This grandmother she insulted was the one who stood up for me when I was being bullied. There was no way I was going to sit there and not say anything. I looked her in the face and said, "You don't have a mirror now, do you?"

Infuriated, she responded, "Get out of my classroom."

There I stood in the intense sun, away from my lesson. Suddenly, I saw the principal approaching. I knew that every child sent outside was mercilessly beaten with a leather strap. I already felt beaten down from my illness and now being put out.

The classroom door was held open by a huge four-inch hook. Without a second thought, I slipped between the door and that hook. While suffering from hepatitis, I had lost a tremendous amount of weight and easily stood there undetected until the lunch bell rang. I then slipped from behind the door and fell in line with the other children as we left the school grounds for lunch.

Later, my teacher told me that because for my many absences, she was considering holding me back. However, after the common entrance results were revealed, she couldn't, because I had the seventh highest score in her class. Only one of her students earned the coveted scholarship, and I was not that person.

As an adult, I have experienced anxiety from being around people who display even a hint of bias, whether their actions are directed at me in jest or as overt racism. I prefer to be in places where I am fully loved and accepted. I don't think it is healthy for me to be where I am not wanted.

I've developed a pseudo strength that often collapses at the first hint of prejudice. It feels like I'm propped up by an everlasting hope that fails me at the most crucial moments, like fainting every time I need to take a stand. Time and time again, I have been left to confront the fiercest battles, alone, draining my capacity to defend myself when it matters most. This relentless solitude has eroded my resilience, leaving me vulnerable in critical moments where strength and support are paramount. So, I lash out when frustrated, and then retreat to a place of safety where I stumble on, yet I am acutely aware that I am missing out on the rewards of boundless living.

# REFLECTION

The paradox of my life lies in my instinct to protect myself from pain, which simultaneously confines me to a life devoid of the richness and vibrancy that comes from engaging fully with the world around me. Whether it's seeking medical care or mending fractured relationships, the journey towards restoration is fraught with challenges, and with longings. Yet, facing these trials, has enabled me to reclaim agency over my life.

My poems, while they chart my path to wellness, also give voice to cries of people yearning for love and acceptance in the face of indifference. They capture the longing of a community to be respected and seen as worthy. My hopes is that my words gets the entire planet to that place of reassurance, that it results in a kinder more accepting world than the one that currently is.

# FROM CHILDHOOD CERTAINTY TO ADULT-ANXIETY

# PERSONAL SIGNIFICANCE

My neighbor's burden,
Why is that of significance?
I cannot see its complexities.
It has no bearing on me.

If tyranny exists in another country,
Within a random family,
If a stranger's grief stricken,
Why should I meddle?

Are the crazy and homeless
Truly voiceless, the poor hopeless,
Prostitutes more victims than criminals?
Aren't there others in authority?
Why should every bystander care,
take notice?

Tragedy without warning,
Stirs the affected to action.

I recall the holocaust,
Tiananmen Square, Colorado, nine-eleven,
The Boston marathon.
Wished someone intervened.

# ENVISION CHANGE!

World's saturated with wonderment,
Inspiration, drunk with merriment.

With bountiful beauty,
It's crippled by ugly.

The hurt igniting places,
Burying truth under ashes.

Till the ruined are reconstructed,
World would be affected.

Open your eyes to it,
Envision change!

# DR. KING'S DREAM

Doctor King's dream was clear,
but the police don't seem to care.
Blacks are still treated unfair.
We don't need to shed another tear.

There are riots in the streets.
I wonder if we'll ever live in peace.
It's like a repeat of the sixties.
Some of them will be arrested.

It doesn't matter if we're yellow or brown.
We don't need to be gunned down.
So, drop your weapons y'all.
Another brother doesn't need to fall.

Some say there's improvement,
We don't need the civil rights movement.
Obama became President,
but I say that's irrelevant.

All lives matter but consider the facts.
Who's being beaten and shot in the back?
At age 14 Emmett Till shouldn't be dead.
Or should Samuel DuBose be shot in the head.

24 unarmed black men killed in 2015.
All shot by police; though a gun wasn't seen.
David Felix died for stealing a purse.
Many go unpunished for doing far worse.

Anthony Hill was an air force vet.
Shot and died because of mental illness.
Charly Keunang was homeless.
Shot multiple times and died regardless.

# FIGHT!

Let your voice be your chosen weapon.
Not guns that cause destruction.
Pursue objective through negotiations,
Devastation's not a solution.

Speak, don't retaliate or destroy
Property, respect life;
don't take it from others.

Put away your guns; and be heard
through words, fight!

The listener's not enslaved
Eventually he hears. Stay open minded,
Don't become blinded, consumed,
swallowed up by despair.
Struggle ends as awareness rises.

# EVERY PARENT'S DREAM

If all shed outer layering,
Our hunger's the same.
Not only for meat and bread,
to succeed and get ahead.

Aim may be different,
collectively the dream's exact,

For children to live well,
to not lack, or be harmed,

to be proud of their accomplishments,
Not for the appearance of prosperity,

the reality. To be surrounded by enablers,
in great and difficult circumstances.

# WALK TO THE US

From dehydration,
Mere thirst they die.
Chance for a better life.

Though treacherous,
Many walk to the US.

Without documentation,
they sneak in,
needing shelter, safety, employment.
Ignorant of cost and consequence,

It's not the dream, they receive,
detention camp placements.
Whatever their peril,
Some will be deported,
Only to start the journey again.

# WORLD WITHOUT BORDER

Is this a singular planet?
World without borders?

Survives with a conscience
or birth without one?

For convenience
some are nurtured, others denied.

Separated by Economy,

Discriminated against by excuses,
invalid reasons: sexuality, origination,
beliefs and color.

It listens to its sons,
gives a deaf ear to its daughters.

Forgives a handful, destroy others.

Why continue to allow intolerance to thrive?
As long as there is life,
Borders should be destroyed.

# BRING DOWN THE CURTAIN OF INDIFFERENCE.

Put an end to that era.
Not that we'd forget.
so, that it may not start over.

Though in our souls we carry pain,
Mourn the loss of our brothers,
Put an end to this foolish chapter,
So, we may love and stop hurting others.

Bring down the curtain of indifference.
That we may embrace diversity,
Work to change the future for generations
To come.

Bring down the curtain of indifference,
that we may live in peace.
The things that affect our neighbor,
May not impact us presently,
but they could later on.

# HOME

Home builds our foundation in life
Determines thought process,
Gives peace or bring confusion to us.

Home builds confidence or creates doubt,
Forms an empathetic or uncaring person,

Determines quality and state of relationship,
Dictates who we could and cannot be with,
Enables us to love, be kind, accepting of others.

Teaches us how to interact,
Makes us unshakable, independent,
confident, form our philosophies.

More than just a dwelling,
home shape lives and form communities.

# CONSTANT HAGGLE

The Constant haggle for enterprise,
To live like kings and queens
Has caused men to lose morality,
Accept the obscene, freely
give their bodies to be known
for their pursuits.
Rankings reduced to who's doing who.
Righteousness no longer rewarded,
having the right skin and hair's a must.
There is no focus on devotion or gaining trust.
Painted nails and lips' classy, natural beauty
discarded, error's celebrated for television ratings.
Whoredom's now the way to make money,
though there's no security in these endeavors.

# BORN TO LIVE A LIE

Being ethnically ambiguous, I've been
Loved, accepted and denied.

I could be
A "Token friend," proof of inclusiveness
And diversity, and when I am,
that wounds me deeply.

No one's born to live a lie.

Most rather their truth be dignifying.
Not disdain even if that's the standard,

Few would volunteer to be the social putty for change.

Many died that I could live my truth,
So that my ambiguity wouldn't be used,
And differences would not be an issue.

# GOOD GIRLS,

I admit you try,
But drop the act, you're wise.
You got that smile that beams.
You go to good extremes.

Good girls leave no trace,
Erasing memories that linger,
Building walls pretty high,
Pretending everything's alright.

Good girls dance with purity,
Twirling in a world of fantasy.
Basking actions like they're crowns,
Not letting life tear you down.

Drowning sorrows with laughter,
Chasing happy ever after,
Holding secrets deep inside,
Fighting battles that you hide.

Good girls sing songs in whispers,
Afraid of being heard by listeners.

Good girls, when in
search for love,
longs for a prince
who's way above,
That he will be the
change they seek,
The release from her
ball and chain.

To all the good girls out there,
I'm preaching to the choir.
Let your voice be heard aloud,
Not in whispers, not in doubt.
Find your power, shine
like a beacon.

# UNCERTAINTY

Labeled and judged,
dysfunctional, rebellious,
Angry, demanding and loud,

Neglected from conception,
I'm society's rejection,

They often blame,
point and call names.

Ignore, refuse to accept,
I didn't choose to be.

But who's responsible?
Is it me, my genes?
Others around me?

All who ignored,
Didn't help or try to cure?

The law doesn't contemplate,
Or the world empathizes, recognize,
the wounded, where there are victims.

# INDIFFERENCE

A call for comfort, assistance,
met by retaliatory words.

Who are you, presumptuous girl?
You are last, my selection's first,
Your cries don't have to be heard.

Footstool of rejection
Echoed those words.

More important were defense,
Not displaying concern,
and I was gifted with avoidance.

Lost a withering friendship
that never truly blossomed,

Was labeled as having emotional struggles,
Refused assistance as a minority person.

# BROTHER: I GET YOUR SEETHING ANGER.

Realizing not helping you escape your prison was no
different from leaving you to be consumed by fire.

I see that stealing from a struggling being is a level of
indifference that speaks profoundly, shows a heart that's frozen.
It illustrates a lack of affection, shouts I don't care.

With no admission of wrongdoing, the fashion of this
world is to not take responsibility, to never say sorry.
The slave-master model continues.

The drum I hear whispers:
a historic genocidal cruelty,
continuous generational injury,
historical tales of inaccuracies,
the in your face,

Blame, shame and hostility,
irradiated some swiftly,
Blamed you for the crimes of the villain.

Had there been love,
Had your burden not been,
Had your path been easy,
Your life would have continued.

Brother,
Love shelters,

Understands,
Doesn't stray or turn away,
It feels your pain,
Fights for truth.

As others blindly follow,
Take the day's narrative as fact,
Lives with shadows of deception.

In the heart where love resides,
A light shines unwavering,
A beacon in the darkness,
Guiding lost souls,
to the sanctuary of truth.

# BOOMERANG!

People are more precious
than things they own.
Shouldn't be picked up,
put down like a phone.

They can be fragile,
handle with care,
don't cast them off,
as if beyond repair.

Unlike a dress or a shoe,
People have potentials,
and shouldn't be labeled.

Life has a way of coming around,
they can become the toast of the town.

Then boomerang knocks a skeptic down.

# FOUNDATION OF PEACE

All panic over that or this,
and do whatever it takes to achieve
desire and dreams but push aside
what should be cherished.

It's not fancy cars or designers' jeans,
but relationships with others.

By loving more, we discriminate less,
For love is the foundation of peace.
If all had love, what more would any need?

# TO ALWAYS BE,

because freedom birth me,

Determined because hope nursed me,
Poised I stand with dignity,
Believing goodness watches over me.
Confident that mistakes do not hold me captive,
Or obligated to give in, because motivation's
The boost that gave me my ranking.

# MOTHER

Her who bore me never loved or held me.
She who chose me; I loved, but didn't want.
Left me empty, longing for affection.
For love, true desire, my yearning lingered on and on.
I gave myself to countless men longing to be filled.
It was not for enjoyment; I was addicted to fixing myself.
Preoccupied, I needed relief, answers. Who was I,
a wanted or a throw away child?
That was my struggle, the need I tried to rectify.
I wanted to feel accepted, for life to be better.
Was aware of people's views, and opinions of me.
By my perception, confusion, understanding,
I long for these things not to be. I was
her chosen child and she loved me a great deal.

# THE CRY OF OUR CHILDREN

signifies life's first
and last breath,
birth and death,
on these we reflect.

The pinnacle of success,
After a fall, first steps,
Pain from hardship,
When needs are unmet.

In happiness, times of regret,
For our children,
others we've never met,

We cry when saddened,
Earn freedom, winnings,
At start, in-between and endings.

Whatever the reason,
The cry of our children,
Should never go unattended.

# HATRED

Hatred as drizzle,
Chisels at human souls.

Contrives a crevice to separate them,
Deceives and ensnares its surroundings.

Fear and heartache are its weapons,
Vindictiveness the float it parades on.

Discouragement its cathartic instruction,
Defeating the strongest of men.

Wears masks of love, protection,
guardian, not an enemy but a friend.

Many are its victims: Those with opinions,
The faithful, most vulnerable,

It demolishes and wounds people.
Nations crumble to devastation.

Hatred's robust, yet uplifts no one.

Constantly without regret, awards wrong,
Inflicts, curses its very subjects,

Most destructive weapon to exist.

# LOVE SHOULD BE EMBRACED.

Like a beautiful awakening,
a flower bud that's opening.
welcomed by a heart that's willing.

Like a child with open arms,
Showered on by snow that's falling.
So, should we react to love.
Like gentle giants' caring for
a fragile gift that shouldn't be crushed.

# NO COMFORT OR REWARD

Pressures from heartache
laid on my chest.
All I wanted was rest.

To seek out the healer
Of all these things,

while he closed his eyes.

I labored for the homeless.
Not desiring compassion,
admiration from any,
just he who refused me.

As if there could be
reward, comfort
in him who turned away
in my day of trouble,
I say, there was none.

# I NEED TO GO TO REHAB

Tho' I can't afford it.
I've got a Louis Vuitton bag,
I've got some designer shoes.
I've a few dollars in credit,
rehab can lessen my pain.

I'd give up my designer things.
I'd give up anything to not feel.
And whoever is judging me,
I'd give them my crazy, if I could transfer it.

I need to go to rehab, I can't lift my arm.
There's no medication or fix,
No medics to help me lift it.
I need to get my strength back,
therapy could help me with this.

I've trouble getting up from sitting.
I tell myself calm down.
Your doctor will give you psychotropics.
I need to go to rehab, it's not only for addicts.

# BLINDED BY GRIEF,

Bewildered by events.
Gloominess hid her radiant eyes.
Coldness emitted from her lifeless stare.
Blood still surging through could not repair
Her broken heart.
Aspirations vaporized in her collapsing world.

Those around, as if dazed, closed their eyes.
Church bells continued to chime at sunrise,
dogs howled interrupting the stillness of night.
Families continued to gather, welcoming new life,

She lived for what she long to be.
Could not accept chaos, her loss,
embrace fate; find joy in what defeated her.
Chose to comfort in sorrow.

# ALL IS WELL

All would be well,
Blissful and cured!
If my will could make it so.

All gruesomeness,
Sickness and death
Would succumb to treatment.

Distress, automatically vanquished!

People's heart would never stop
But always beat.

Fountain of wellness would saturate bodies.
Illness would retreat,
Never rob another life.

There would be no need to weep.
All would rise up and find peace.
Bodies would miraculously be regenerated.

# VICTORY WORTH KNOWING.

Victory, I long to claim,
To be entangled with
As the reward of effort.

I desire to soak in triumph,
Be free from condemnation.

Although to experience stillness,
There had to be a time of tiredness,
But from harshness, I wish to be insulated.

Conquest, where do you live?
How do I connect with you?
Is that by choice or selection?

Wish you'd answer me,
restore my beauty, give me peace,
Acknowledge that I need relief.

# SURVIVORS WIN

At the pinnacle of life great things happen,
Though losing battles can discourage.
Condition your mind to stay encouraged.

The impossible is something to tackle,
Though setbacks can be a hassle.

Through persistence achievements gained.
Whatever missing can be earned,
Even when bombard by negative concerns,

A winner's inside everyone,
but it takes effort to unveil him.

A champion continuous effort,
proves critics wrong, being pliable
change situation. Through listening
knowledge's obtained.

Life teaches many great lessons,
but it takes experience to be profound.
Survivors win but warriors don't always endure.

# RED, WHITE AND BLUE
# THAT YOU DEFEND

I saw the tears as they rolled down her cheeks.
She stretched out her hands but didn't speak.
Who was she? I couldn't remember.
But I didn't want to offender her.

She walked over and kissed my cheek.
She wasn't shy but I felt weak.
I had bandages on my head,
And this is what she said.

Red, white and blue, that you defend,
Star spangled banner I'm your friend.
I'll stand by you, 'til the end,
Because you're my champion.

American hero, I love you,
Though they say, you've lost a limb or two.
You may have challenges at home,
But you won't have to face them alone.

I wanted to turn away, right then,
But I needed her to visit again.
The blast was echoing in my head,
And I wondered why I wasn't dead.

# KING SOLOMON'S BEAUTY

Wish that only one woman could complete me.
I wouldn't have committed to as many.
Yet, I often dreamed of one special lady.
Apparently, we were never meant to be.

Similar to King Solomon's beauty,
She was dark mysterious and lovely.
I thought she was the one for me
Even now, her memory consumes me.

Having many women became my hobby.
Still, I kept thinking of her curvy body.
I saw her waist and breast like jewels.
Addicted to her images I became cruel.

I compared all my women to her,
Even to Hollywood divas in high heels.
She appeared to be more beautiful in sandals,
And that only helped to fuel her appeal.

# BOODILICIOUS LADY

The world needs to know, I'm lovin her.
She's a boodilicious lady.
And still is after having my baby.
'N she's photographed more than any leading lady.
More than any princess or Hollywood actress.

I don't mean to brag, but look at her.
My girl got curves.
Her hip swings and her bottom swerves.
It doesn't matter what she wears.
She's the woman that I prefer.

And though they're all lookin,
They're trying to see if I fit in.

I'm proud of her and all that she does,
That no one prints.
And to my woman I'm a prince,
And to me, she defines beauty,
'N we're the greatest love story.

# HEAVEN MUST HAVE SENT YOU.

I was living as if nothing but heartache mattered.
Trapped in wishes and all that couldn't be.
I longed for a life that was easy.
Giving love but not feeling loved completely.

Heaven must have sent you.
Cause when you walked in my life
There wasn't anything I wanted anymore.
Heaven must have sent you
Cause nothing missing deep inside.
I have all the love I was longing for.

I wasn't chasing fame or reaching for glory,
But all I worked for had faded from view.
That stole my heart and left me needy,
'til I was wanted, loved deeply by you.

My days are now filled with joy and beauty.
Having love has altered my story.
I'm no longer focusing on pain,
or have any need to worry again.

*(This is a song lyric in the Songs by Ruth collection)*

# LAMBORGHINI

Oo, you look like eye candy,
Good looking and all that.
Who wouldn't want to be with you?
It would be like driving a Lamborghini.
I'd take you for a spin more than I need to.
I'd go for a drive, to be seen with you.

I don't have to be the one in the driver's seat,
Life's not always about who's behind the wheel.
But where the journey takes me.
Everywhere I go, I'd take you,
to spend quality time with you,
I'd devise a reason to drive.

You'd surely be my favorite car.
The make and model that I want.
Attracting people in the streets,
Looking fresh, like you're custom built.
I'd be pumped up form the oo's and ah's,
I wouldn't care if I'm not steering from my seat.

Nobody should critique the spark we feel.
You meet my need to get away.
You take me places that wouldn't be fun going alone.
Though with my own wheels, I could go anywhere on my own.

# LOVE SONG

Don't let anybody tell you who to love.
There's no rules for who you should fall for.
You can be different from someone.
But energized when you're together.
Love can make a broken heart feels new.
It brings differences together perfectly.

Love can be seen in the eyes.
It's a banner for what's felt on the inside.
It's a big bright toothy smile.
It ignores flaws and issues.
Oh, Yes, that's what love does.
It brings lonely hearts out of exile.

Desire lifts you up, not put you down.
It doesn't deflate you like a balloon,
You know in your gut when it's for real.
It may not be your first but second pick,
But when it's authentic, you know it.
Unlike fake emotions love holds its appeal.

Love is like a glow that sparkles.
An energy that helps you move.
It could be in your midst and you don't know
A soft spot that blossomed into love.

# FOOT PRINTS IN THE SAND

I saw your footprints in the sand
And I wanted to hold your hand.
So, I tried to run after you.
I wanted to have a talk.
I had this need to feel brand new,
So, you and I could walk, together.

Would you please help me?
I want to be well again.
I heard you made a blind man see,
I don't want to complain,
But I need you to heal me.

Running in sand isn't easy.
The wind can be very breezy,
That can hold back the fastest feet,
And I've honestly tried.
Would you please wait so we could meet?
I wish to be at your side, forever.

# UNSTOPPABLE

I said some things I shouldn't have.
I cursed the woman I had chosen.
I lost her and out on love,
And I became broken.

I couldn't tell her I was wrong,
And didn't want to keep reliving,
Just wanted our hurt to heal,
And to know that I was forgiven.

She was black but I was not,
So, I couldn't openly love her.
She married another man.
I felt our friendship was over.

I wish to hold her in my arms,
Although that seem impossible.
I'm living without her and love.
I'm a wreck that's unstoppable.

# IT'S NOT PERSONAL.

It's the way that I am.
Know you think I messed up.
That I'm a pathetic sham.

I wasn't there, when you needed me,
And didn't say sorry for being me
But in my heart, I wanted to,
But didn't know what I could do.

I do want you to understand.
My actions weren't intentional.
I didn't mean to put you last,
But know that's all in the past.

From now on, I'll be there for you.
'N I'll prove that I truly love you.
Not that life will be perfect,
But our time apart you'll forget.

# THE BRAVE

It's true that when it rains it pours,
And your heart feels it can't take much more.
Know that you can survive any storm.
Don't punish yourself when somebody does you wrong.
People often don't come clean about mistakes.
Life's a stage where we all learn to perform.

Be strong, know the brave takes a stand.
Just like Malala, a woman from Pakistan.
Be strong, know the brave unravel lies
And bravery is important to take a stand in life.

Not every wrong can be made right,
Justice fades with each passing daylight.
You don't have to stay victimized.
Live your life well, don't give up or die.
Just fight, fight, fight with all of your might.
You are worthy a hundred million times.

Get up, go out and show your strength.
Just be prepared to go the full length.
We don't pick our trials that chose us.
Some battles are yours, not for anyone else.
Oh, you do need to act when destiny calls.
Change won't come if you do nothing at all.

*(The Brave is a song lyric in the songs by Ruth music collection.)*

# TRUE HERO

One day I'll answer you.
I'll explain why I avoided you.
It wasn't because of how you were,
But my need to feel secure.

I wrestle within me to be
But kept my conflict low key.
So if you can live without me,
Then move on, and be free.

If a person doesn't love himself,
Then he can't anyone else.
Mr. Right would've fought for you,
But I didn't try to hold unto you.

We can no longer pretend.
I didn't treat you like a friend.
My actions caused you distress,
Robbed you of happiness.

One day the world will know,
Not I, but you were a true hero.
I didn't help but tried to keep you down,
But joy and honor will be your crown.

# PASSION'S POWER

All the doings of a man get tested,
even the love he gives and receives,
But if you ever hurt in love. It'll be OK.
The sting of love's better than no love any day.

If you ever feel like giving up,
Remember,
Passion gives power to the faint.
If you want to quit altogether,
Consider,
Passion's many things, but a quitter it aint.

Love's the story behind many smiles.
It can heal the broken and fragile.
So, when you love do so with sincerity,
And trust that love will last and lasts eternally.

We lose interest in the familiar,
Become insensitive and don't care,
But love can revive somebody's heart and spirit.
Return a spark after the embers of love has vanished.

# I'M LIVING MY DREAMS!

Hey Beautiful, how was your day?
Your smile took my breath away.
I love those lips of yours.
I could stare at them for hours.

I thought I was having a dream.
We looked like we were a team.
All I had became ours,
And our love opened many doors.

You fell for my boyish charms,
'N rested peacefully in my arms.
I knew I was captured.
I found my happily ever after.

I'm living my reality.
Some think it is all a fantasy,
But my lady's here besides me,
And life is as it should always be.

# SEPTEMBER

She said her name was September,
And her name I could always remember,
And I'd think about her in the fall.
She was long legged and tall.
We ran high school track together.
I told myself I'd marry her.
We'd be like Flo and Al Joyner.

But my name she doesn't recall.
I said hello, she didn't answer at all.
I saw her driving a fancy car.
She was now a movie star.
We lived in a very small town.
Instead of a smile, I got a frown.
She rolled her eyes and then looked down.

I have to buy magazines to see her smile,
But I've been loving her for quite a while.
How could she not know me now?
I need to remind her somehow.

September, September,
Would you please turn around?
September, September,
Remember when we used to run!
September, September,
Call me when you're ready to settle down.

# I USE WHAT I HAVE

Whether pain or joy,
for if it weren't for ache,
I'd have no romanticism.

If not for emptiness,
I wouldn't love.

If not for desire,
I'd grow weary of failure.
I'd be a wall flower,
Not a creator, if not for a thought.

I use what I have,
Words, and my imagination.
I create romantic moments
And lamentation, without a lover.

# BURNING BRIDGES

I wouldn't listen to what she had to say.
I had better things to do with my day.
Sometimes her words cut like a blade.
I ignored the many calls she made.

I've never been one for burning bridges.
I'm not the kind to cut all ties.
But she just isn't going to let me let go,
So, I'm burning this bridge tonight.

Many times, she's called me uncaring and vain.
She did that time and time again.
I'm the gentleman I've always been,
But she's determined to get under my skin.

I wish her well with love 'n all her dreams,
But I wouldn't fall for her extremes.
When we were young I admired her.
I was her friend but not her lover.

# CUTS ME IN TWO

It hurts to talk to you.
The way you talk to me,
Now I'm feeling blue.
Who do I talk to
Now that you're gone.

I need to love me more.
You left me broken unloved.
Now I need to restore,
Who I was before.

In loving you, you cut me in two
That taught me,
I should do this for me,
not do as you do
left me there in two.
To me you feel nothing
And you never did,
But for me to heal,
I need to love me more
You, left me there in two,
You got me shaking  and different,
but I'm going to love me more.

And who would want you now then?
They must be crazy.
Who would love you like I did.
Those hurtful words,
I.. won't let you break me.

I... need to love more.
You left me broken unloved
Now I need to restore.
Who I was before.

On my way back home,
I'm still so confused.
I was so alone.
Whilst I was next to you,
like babe, it took me so long to move.
I need to love me some more,
you left me broken unloved.
Now I need to restore
Who I was before.

*(Cuts Me In Two is a song lyric, song is in the Songs by Ruth app, Collection)*

# A PLACE OF LOVE

I'll take you to a place of love,
There diamond isn't the measure.
There's be no more doubt,
And you'll be my greatest treasure.

Don't take your eyes off me.
I'll be your best partner.
I'll love you more than your mother.
And be better to you than any brother.

I know that the past matters,
But I'll stay for better or worse,
Although I've lived life in reverse.
You will always be my first.

I'll gladly take care for you,
And loving you should be easy.
You're the emerald that completes me,
And we'll both be very happy.

*(A Place of love was recorded by an autistic friend but
the song is not apart of the Songs by Ruth Collection)*

# THINGS WE NEED TO DISCUSS

I don't need a love that's like magic,
Or one that blows like a volcano,
And I've to fight to gain control,
That hurts 'n grieves me to my bones.

I want to always be myself.
Not dazzled by anyone's spell.
I need a love that treats me well,
Not one that's played out in a hotel.

And if that's the way we'll be,
The world would see you got me.
Nothing could come between us,
But these things we need to discuss.

I don't want to be a seasonal chick.
I want a secure relationship.
Not one that's fast and ends quick,
But one that's worth sticking with.

It's not that things would be perfect,
Or that we wouldn't get upset,
But that we'd be the best fit yet,
And not question why we connect.

# TIGHT FITTED JEANS

I first saw you dressed in tight fitted jeans.
I couldn't accept what my mind was thinking.
Wished I could touch those buns of steel,
Instead, I stood still 'n ignored my feeling.

You took my breath away dressed like that,
And I thought I was going to explode,
But the next day I saw you kissing a blonde.
Two weeks later caressing another woman.

The moment we met, I was so turned on.
I wanted to give in to temptation,
I wished to walk beside you as my man.
I had to fight to control my emotion.

That interaction taught me a lesson.
It takes time to get to know a person,
And good looks aren't everything,
So, I'm no longer hooked by first impression.

# IF ONLY

I'm not the kind of girl who talks much.
Lately, I've been writing non-stop.
I met a man, 'n I started to open up.
He was a great dresser 'n a heart throb.

I waved at him; he smiled and winked.
I dreamed we became romantic.
We went on a European vacation.
And on a cruise across the Atlantic.

We'd often pass by each other,
'N I'd think about what could happen,
But I knew he was probably thinking,
I'm just a teen on the streets of Manhattan.

If only we were friends.
All I *imagined would be real.*
And "if only" I could tell him.
Dairy, that would be ideal.

I would run barefooted in the rain,
And splash water on the pavement.
It wouldn't be fun, if I had shoes on,
But he shook his head in amazement.

He doesn't see all I will be,
And doesn't seem to know how I feel.
It shouldn't matter that I'm eighteen.
So maybe, he's not the one for me.

# I CAN SEE CLEARLY THAT,

I placed my hopes for love in made up stories.
I'd imagined them when I was sad,
But love built on lies don't last.
They get buried in the past.

My thoughts are clearer now.
My hurt will soon heal.
I'll be lifted up somehow,
No matter how torn I feel.

My mind might rewrite all memories of love.
It might correct all the wrongs.
It might replace its heart of stone,
And give love a softer one.

I believed love was tender and kind.
That allure drew me.
Captivated, I was blind,
I didn't grasp perfect love was hard to find.

# A QUESTION FOR LOVE.

Love, why did you disguise yourself?
The years chipped away. Gave me heartache,
Changed my perspective.

I hypothesized:
Desire died, made a maneuver,
Left me with ideal ideas:

Loving lasts forever, cradles,
Doesn't suffocate, or causes agony.
Gives freely, compromises,
is empathetic, open, and recognizable.

Shouldn't have to ask, earn,
Appear inferior to affection,
But like an eagle soar high,
as should love's recipients.

# A MESSAGE FOR LOVE

I ached to hear your voice,
sit spell bound in your presence.
To be cradled by your embrace,
comforted by your arms, patiently
I waited, anticipated your arrival.

You turned away, let me down.
I felt alone and abandoned.

Wanted our moment to be a song
heard all over the world,
not as rock and roll,

the anthem of lovers. Desired,
though it was not always so.

# STORY BOOK OF LOVE

music and lyrics,

Composed to romance audiences,
Played on and off performance stages.

When heard captivate strangers.

One of kindness and concern, dance
portrayed in melody and words.

Collaboration of poet,
And musician, committed,
Entangled by their composition.

Crafted through diligence,
not achieved in an instant.

All's enthralled with their story
and production.

# THE THOUGHTFUL SPOUSE,

Calls to say he'll be late.
Leaves a hand-written note that says you're loved.
Displays gratitude, does not take his partner for granted.
Allow days when nothing is required or expected.
Support endeavors, career choices, does not criticizes,
Takes time to understand weakness or illnesses.
Comforts when necessary, displays concern.
Send thoughts that say he's there in spirit.
Is never too busy to listen, does to benefit family, not self.
Makes no excuses but accepts responsibility.
Is able to say sorry and make amends.

# WORDS ALONE

As if words of love could stand alone,
Give shelter and feed me.

Days when I was hungry, he fed,
Provided for another family,
But spoke and boasted about me.

Cold nights caused me to shiver.
No furious fire could warm me.

He sucked the energy
That gave me my radiance;
My soul grew dim.
No other could ignite me.

Song of brokenness and shame,
The anthem of my life.

Daggers that wounded, his words;
Could never fill the gaping hole
created. That escaped what he stated.

He professed eternal love for me,
With his words alone.

# IT'S A WOMAN'S THING

To be strong and emotionally vulnerable,
To march to her own rhythm,
And to still be taken in by her lover.

It's a woman's thing
To accept her man as her equal and also her hero.
To be in and out of step with him,
To hold on and to let go when she needs to.

It's a woman's thing,
A woman's thing to be and do as she choose to.
A woman's thing to be fashionable,
or homely, if that's what she wishes to do.

# MAN OF MY DREAMS

I didn't want a man I could tame,
But one who'd support my aim.
The one I loved no longer cares.
Believed my job was to support his career.

He'd always shift the blame,
And claim to love me the same.
I spent stressful days on my own,
Believing our place was not a home.

I was a lovely woman to look at.
At first, he told other men that.
Things changed after we had kids.
He broke my heart with his many digs.

He was not as charming as before.
My prince became a Lion that roared,
And life's not adventurous as it were.
Still, I craved the man that I adored.

# SMOKY MIRRORS

This is how it is inside my bubble.
He and I aren't the perfect couple.
He says he cares about me, I say he doesn't.
His words hold me but his arms fumbles.
Our friends see the pictures we pose for.
Nobody knows what really was or wasn't.

He says this is the same o, same o.
Like happy is not what we aim for.
On a cycle, we do what we've done before.
Our mood's either sweet or sour,
Hard to fix 'n difficult to deal with.
We keep holding on when we need to let go.

Our love is filled with errors.
Errors for which sorry isn't the cure.
Sorry can't wipe certain hurts off,
things can still be seen in smoky mirrors.

# A MILLION TIMES

How would you know to miss me?
You acted as if you didn't need me.
Loving you was my greatest regret:
I don't know how I got caught in your net.

I've asked myself a million times,
And every time the answer was the same:
You would never be my refuge,
Relying on you was like depending on Ebeneezer Scrooge.

My heart was enslaved by your words,
But sweet words were all you ever gave.
I won't bother repeating them,
They don't have value like they're gems.

My hurt and my pain are now gone,
And I can now walk away and move on.
That's why I'm no longer complaining;
Each day, my thoughts of you are waning.

# LOVE'S SECRET

Loyalty where there's hurt
is that sincerely honest, should any
cling when love's shattered?

Continue as though all's OK,
Keep up appearances while hiding truth?

Are there advantages to being faithful
to one who isn't?
One who keeps "love" a closely guarded secret?

If love were an undiscovered garden,
any could explore it.

A secret ingredient in a recipe,
It could be made, tasted and savored.

If none other than our hearts knew,
goes wild in its presence,

in anticipation of the world knowing,
without love professing the same,

it would be a fantasy, unknown,
not photographed or fulfilled,
but exists only in our mind.
So many stick with the tangible.

# LOVE ISN'T GIVING IN

Every time I think of you,
The tears begin to rain.
If I get you back,
I'll won't let go again.
I regret that I sent you away,
But since that day,
I've gotten on my knees and prayed.

Love isn't giving in or settling.
It's falling down and holding on.
It's growing in each other's arms.
Love should be expressed, not withdrawn.

I've had my lessons in love,
And in losing I've learned.
When everyone leaves,
true love always returns.
When I think of you,
I consider these things,
'N my promise to put you on eagle's wings.

If you're believing my love is a hurricane,
I can't say that's loving, if I brought you shame.
I'll have to make changes, so you can be secure.
We all need love, 'n it shouldn't be obscure.

# NOT GOING TO BREAK ME!

I kept turning the other cheek.
And you walked all over me.
You didn't give me a chance to speak.
But you're not gonna break me.

I always do my best to bend.
But you seem to never give in.
There's no debate you'd always win.
But you're not gonna break me.

I can't take the fights.
Or you coming home drunk at nights.
I don't wanna kiss you, but you make me,
But you're not gonna break me.

Everything you said was fake.
I put up with more that I could take.
I cried so hard sometimes I'd shake.
But you're not gonna break me.

No, there hasn't been another man.
I don't care if you don't understand.
I'm moving out as fast as I can.
But you're not gonna break me.

# TO PUT ME BACK TOGETHER

I still love you but I don't need you now.
I waited a long time for you to change.
There's no point saying that from now on, you'll care.
All that matters, is for a long time we got nowhere.

I don't have to prove anything to you.
All I wants to be who I use to be.
Me loving me is the key to reclaim myself.
I got to put me back together.
You don't see I'm splintered,
Or do you know that I became someone else.

I don't have the things you've done written down.
These errors came between us.
I don't need to be reminded.
I know you don't agree with my responses.
My hurt won't be mended with you next to me.
When we're together I'm surrounded.

It doesn't matter what you did, my desire got me lifted,
You not loving me was not a crime you hid.
But God forbids the anger that's in me.
That needs to fade.
*(This is a song lyric in the songs by Ruth collection)*

# THE HEART REVEALS A LOT ABOUT A PERSON,

It shows intent, the core of who a person is.
Still, no one should ignore what the heart feels,
especially when there are grievances.
The heart knows how things ought to be done,
That expectation can cause one to feel let down,
But as the heart reacts, we have to live with its response.

The opinion of others doesn't matter,
If the heart does not agree,
Whether the issue is love, life or destiny,
The heart knows what should and shouldn't be.

# RHYTHM AND BLUES

How could I stay with you?
You act as if I shouldn't be,
Shouldn't have an opinion
and have no right to speak.

No woman's that helpless.
But you're a control freak.

Love has many rhythms.
It may not always be sultry and smooth,

But a rhythm that centers around rules,
repeat measures and doesn't improve
is redundant and not a sweet tune.

A secure woman has her own rhythm.
And when added to another, improves
delivers sounds like an orchestra
during her vibrant years.

If she's dumb down, her beat
sounds like a tuba blown by a novice.
She'd be more captivating in harmony,
with a melody that's in syn with hers.

# PUZZLE PIECES

Put us together like puzzle pieces.
Let us be beautifully linked when completed.
Don't let our desire ever decreases.
We don't want to be lapped sided or unfinished.

No one wants to be cheated from love.
Lift us up, but don't put any of us down.
We don't wish to fall, but to fly like doves.
All desire stability but none wants to drown.

Lovers should complement their companion.
People should fit as if they're made for each other.
All wants to have a great union.
No one needs to feel unwanted because of another.

# UNDONE

You meant for me to come undone,
But verbal attacks won't keep me down.
You lied about the lie you lied about,
Now all I want from you is freedom.

I have free will to pick and choose.
I don't need a man to fill my dad's shoes.
I have a career to pursue,
And that is what I'll choose to do.

I'm not less than anybody.
I don't have to take scraps buddy.
Woman doesn't mean secondary.
I'm in charge of my destiny.

Hillary's running for President.
That no Monica could prevent.
I have the same drive as she,
And verbal abuse won't stop me.

# MEN VS BOYS

When boys are seven
they pinch and punch women.
When they are grown, they hug them.
No one wants to be in love with a razor.
Every woman wants a man with controlled behavior.
If we expect bad behavior from men,
That's what they'll give in return.
If we hold them to higher standards,
They'll act accordingly.

# STAND UP TO ABUSE

Recognize the face of abuse,
It's a worldwide phenomenon.
It's your neighbor, coworker, sister,
daughter, Mother, friend.

It's not only physical; it's verbal, sexual and mental.
Anyone who's being used as a source of income,
imprisoned, and mistreated by someone.

Don't hide your face or remain a phantom.
Stand up to abuse, and let it be known.

If it would bring harm to you,
recognize it, but expose the damage
That's been inflicted.

Doesn't matter who it is, was,
did, does or wants to become.
Your life is worth saving.

Stand up to Abuse.
You are not alone.

# LOVED MY BODY:

There were times in life I felt I couldn't win.
Then, I long to numb my pain with gin.
I knew that would have been a mistake,
Even if it took all my troubles away.

I grew up feeling good about the body I was in,
But I also felt the pressures of trying to look thin,
So, I only had a hamburger every now and then,
And I went back to salads and working out again.

Love my body 'n I don't feel less than anyone.
Love my body, though I don'l look like my friends,
Over and over, I kept telling them again,
Stop criticizing; I love the body that I am in.

I'm not a size six but still I'm fit.
They are the ones who couldn't handle it.
I saw it in all their reaction.
They didn't show me any compassion.

It mattered how they made me feel.
It didn't matter, what they believed.
My thick curves were ideal,
But it seems they meant to hurt me.

# STRONG BUT FRAGILE

Beauty comes from within,
Not from skin texture or physique.
Conditioned to believe it's in appearances,
As seen on television, on cover of magazines,
We accept what we are taught as real.

Though it's difficult to block false messages,
All need to learn to ignore external noise.
Don't let any condition get the best of you,
Even when strong, any can be torn down.

# AT THE EDGE OF WATER,

I dreamed not of past love,
one I never heard of.
Desiring that special someone,
A relationship that would never be over,

I would carry our son,
Sing songs to our daughters.
In life challenges
He would not disappoint me.

I desire to start over,
Although I am older.
The lover I've never heard of,
Our times are truly over.

At the edge of water
I stand disappointed.
As the sand shifts under my feet,
My aching heart races within me.
I walk away, though not easily.

# STRENGTH AS SEEN IN WOMEN,

As they face obstacles,
Carry the burden for others.

Make career choices,
Shape and care for future leaders,
Shows beauty of the human spirit.

Displayed through duty,
Lives they've touched,
Encouraged and lifted up.

Even when disheartened,
Unsure, unrecognized,
they keep at it.

Strength as seen in women,
No one should want to change that.

# WOMAN IN THE MIRROR,

Appeal to no one else.

If no other considers you,
Take care of yourself.

Beauty flows from within,
Not opinion of others.

Woman be forthright,
Manage life; don't let it crush you.

You are a unique beauty,
And the way you should be.

# MUTUAL LOVE

A rag played on my feelings,
Called my desire scary,
Severing my affection.

Was not my original,
or last love.
Replacement lover,
After giving up the first,

Displaced my longings,
Settled for one
I did not synchronize with.

Recognized affection
was not one sided,
Satisfying if both expressed it.

# CRUSH

Blush in my face
exposed my yearning,
Tipsy not from alcohol,
the presence of a crush.

With head bowed, eyes lowered,
Not for prayer but shyness,
Yet convinced,
Our future. tied us.

Without the utterance of a word,
A grin blanketing his face.
Certainly, that revealed desire,
Not amusement at my fluster.

A social cue misinterpretation,
I did not realize,
His girlfriend stood behind him
And I was left bewildered.

# LOVE I DESIRED

I searched for the love I desired.
He was nowhere I grew weary.
Distributed but withheld from me, I fainted.
Choose not to advertise my beauty.

Kindness should have been his brand,
Not indifference or harshness displayed by him.
Lived my days with thoughts of love, believing,

*I should have been chosen,*
*quirky as I was,*
*as his perfect woman,*
*Not as his competition,*
*Or servant, but partner.*

Symbolic of our affection,
Nothing should have come before me,
As he stood beside me, and I by him,
We would have completed each other.

# ONLY ONE DANCES

If I could have only one dance,
Would I choose to dance with anyone?
Or a special someone?

Would I dance in my early years?
Delay it for the peak or near sundown?

With whom would I dance,
a lover, stranger or life's partner?

Would I dance when I am weary,
with someone who ignored me,
gave heartache or made me happy?

Would these things affect quality,
thrill of my dance?

Would I be out of step, synchronized
based on partnership, timing I chose?

Should the first or last lover dance,
Or one who chose to romance,
Flatter, love and was kind to me?

Should I choose to dance when I'm strong
would I always be able to stand?

In choosing all needs be considered.

# LOVER OF MY SOUL

My body ached to know.
Doctor declared it a delusion,
I believed it to be so.

Who doesn't know the spirit
needs be as well as the body?

In my confusion, I wondered,
If that physician was a healer,
or just a control addict?

Wished he realized
his words afflicted
my already hurting soul.

I desired contentment,
Not the loss of my support.

My beliefs empowered me,
I did not need to let them go.

# YOU, MORE THAN ANYONE

A superior life some enjoy,
As they live a dazzling life.

Why should I simply survive?
Struggle with inferior life?

Wish to be a typical person,
Not peculiar, rare or different,

to stand out for accomplishments,
Not denied because of inability.

Want it to be said, I defied struggles.

Graduated not only high school,
All that I did could also be commended.

But for now, life's basics top my wish list:
Having a home, medical care,
place I feel safe and cared for,

Not because anyone, but my mother.
Took the time to care.

# HAPPY MONDAY

I heard someone say, happy Monday,
I replied, have a great day.

Even with dreams 'n plans,
The unexpected happens.
Hold on, hold out for better,
But life's in God's hands.

Needs, and wants will always exist,
But try to not give in to weakness.

Happy Monday,
have a pleasant day.
Happy Monday,
Put your struggles away.

Happy Monday,
try to not complain,
Happy Monday,
Live in the moment.

# SELF-EXPRESSION!

Small child weeping,
Reaching for mother,
Agonizing reflection of me.

Eyes showered,
not my body.

Cheeks stained,
not dried or cleaned
like most children's.

Tears flowed like a fountain
'til sorrow was purged,

Ceased not from love or comfort,
But weariness, inability to continue.

# BETTER!

Carefree disposition ended,
when the miserable befriended,
Sweet side devoured.

Mountainous distress conquered,
Anxiety, confusion, and emptiness,
redefined my character.

Mind preoccupied by sadness,
Face a vision of wretchedness.

But need resurrected my aim,
renewed my dying dreams,

I had to be better, rise up,
And not remain angry or bitter,
cast grief off, and put doubt aside.

# GO AWAY

I keep hearing the mean things you said.
Your words keep repeating they play in my head.
I had nowhere to go but you made me wanna hide.
Because of struggles, many days I curled up and cried.

Go away, go away, but don't fill me with shame.
I'm nothing more than a pawn in your game.
Go away, go away, I'm just trying to survive.
But hash words and bullying has claimed many lives.

I didn't want to live life locked in.
You formed your conclusion without question.
You believed I chose to look the way that I do.
I didn't and I wouldn't choose to behave like you.

I'm grown up but inside I'm a kid.
And that doesn't cause some to bat an eyelid.
You need to know that's how it'll always be for me.
With Autism, I'll live and I'll never be really free.
(Go away is a song by Ruth but not in the songs by Ruth collection)

# BROKEN PEOPLE CAN
# BE REPAIRED.

Quick fixes don't change anything,
But understanding makes a difference.
Love breaks barriers down,
As compassion builds resilience.

Many wrongs are hard to make right.
The pain's there when we don't see it.
Life's pleasant for the majority.
But for many it's a struggle,
Undeniable
Break down in society.

# HOW COULD I CHOOSE SOMEONE WHO REJECTED ME?

Someone who walked away
As I cried out, help me!

Someone who left me to die,
Someone who caused me to ask why.

Someone who stood by as I struggled.
How could I, love such a one?
How could I? How could I?

We all deserve unconditional love,
We're all made of flesh and blood.
Skin's just a covering, and ethnicity
Shouldn't determine if one's a thug.

We should regard each other's lives,
not judge without fully knowing.

We all need to care, to forgive, help others,
Not for their benefit, but ours.

We all hurt, so give others a chance,
Not that any is expected to ignore acts of hate,

But no one should ever have to ask,
How could I love someone, who deliberately hates?
How could I, How could I, How could I?

# MY THOUGHTS, MY SAVIOR

On Santa Monica pier
I write poetry, and am amused.

Another plays the blues,
Not my kind of music,
I prefer contemporary tunes.

Santa Monica is my kind of scene.
Few know this aspect of me.

I'm artistic, not a drama queen.
Enjoy losing problems in scenes,
Not being their creator.

Alone, my ideas develop.
With company, they crumble.

My observation, thinking, I savor.
Key to my creativity.

# PLAYING IN THE RAIN

Pitter patter of my own feet
Splashing in water puddles.
Excited as if for the first time
Bare feet met concrete.

Was never drenched until then,
Or felt raindrops upon my head.
Avoided it as if I'd melt.
Didn't see any thrill in getting wet,
Or going shoe-less, until I tried it.

On rainy days, I never played,
Not anything other than board games.
This day a teen cheered me on.
Adults watched from behind misty windows.

# ARTIST'S AIM

The Lyrics the singer sings,
Known poetic writings,
Scripts performed on Broadway,
The unknown poet's longings.

Unlike paintings stored in a garage,
Coveted ones hanging on a museum wall
Is the struggling artist's dream.

The actress serving in a restaurant,
Longs to be discovered,
Even if, the right patron notices.

The desire, dream, hope persists,
Like Doctor Seuss success story,
To be known by every household.

# I CHOOSE LIFE

Gasped for air as if suffocating,
Not that breathing was strenuous,
or I suffering disease,

From responsibility, I carried.
With lips many profess to love me.
Yet blinded to how I was affected.

They explained: it was for me, if I got over it.

The one I loved walked away.
One I despised stayed for a life time.

All these backwards actions caused my reaction.
I caught my breath.

Threw from my mind my regrets
and many wavering emotions
though tumultuous than any ocean.

I wanted to live and breathe easier.

# LIVE, LOVE AND LEARN

Live, love and learn to be thankful.
Every day that you are, be grateful.
No one should focus more on troubles,
But should find joy in what they're given.

Actions reflect who we truly are,
'N thoughts often the leading offender.
Our thinking leads us astray,
Not what others convince us to do or say.

Though no one is perfect,
None should participate in acts of hate,
Or judge others without fully knowing truth.

# GOOD THINGS GIVEN

Good things given to us come from heaven.
'Though things on earth aren't always even.
Christmas gives us a reason,
To share with others, the joy of the season.

Joy doesn't have to be wrapped in a box,
Or does it have to be a visit from St Nicholas,
But a kind act, like the one on that first Christmas.
Give someone the joy of Christmas.

We decorate and light holiday trees.
We celebrate with our families,
But pray that others would find peace,
For the world's conflicts at Christmas time to cease.

Show them more than just the Christmas story,
A king born without wealth or glory,
But true love as displayed by you.
Give someone a reason to celebrate too.

# MISGUIDED,

Path filled with pitfalls,
Life pained by difficulties,
did as expected.

Started as a blank slate,
knew not a better way,
Blamed the universe.

Was not shown, taught,
placed to learn.

Displayed frustration, continued
lost and alone.

Accepted insult as if earned,
Was empty and frustrated.

Fashioned by those around me,
Nurtured by despondency,
Acquired nothing,
believed I couldn't do better.

# LEARNED RESPONSE

Pure as a child's actions,
mimicking what he sees,

Whether complex or simple
as putting on shaving cream,

Repeating ways and dealings,
Of the man who influenced him,

Promoting or building on
Foundation laid out by him,

He will continue, choose to do,
involuntarily as was carried out before him.

# BE MY EXAMPLE

A child today, President the next.
All are capable of climbing
the ladder of success.

Every leader at times needs a lift,
So, build one up that he may be equipped.

If he falls, help him up.
Know that none is perfect,
repetition leads to improvement.

Someday he'll teach another
as he was encouraged to do.
So be a living example.

# QUALITY INVESTMENT

One person can make a difference
Lend a hand for encouragement,
influence others to be kind,
If only with a smile.

People more than fairy tale stories
are fascinating and worth knowing,
closed like an unopened book,
until you dive into them.

Make a difference in someone's life.
Invest in lives more than stocks.

Everyone have the power to be,
to bring about change, impact
views and molding minds.

# MY ACTIONS

Do my actions or my father's
Determine my prospect?

Do his sins or mine
Has lasting effects?

Commit me to uncertainty,
A promising future?

While hurt inflict scars,
Disappointment drives me!

Grief awakens, obstacles delays,
And hindrance strengthens.

If trouble was handed me,
Determination should enable me to flourish.

Attained in the face of hardship.

# HISTORY

Who does History define?
Does it dictate character?
Control attitude, achievement,
Behavior or future?

Should it determine who you'll love?
When to pick, plant or nurture?

History shouldn't discourage,
drive or frame anyone.

Individual choices cause us to move ahead,
Although at times, injustice stalls us.

With togetherness, greater things achieved,
But the past is not anyone's future.

Look forward not behind.
Don't accept error as deserving.

Through individuals' change occurs.
That's what history demonstrates.

# PAPER-MACHE'

I discovered his passion when he was four,
Mixing paper and paste on his bedroom floor.
Never knew what he thought 'cause he couldn't say a word,
But knew how he felt when he made his first bird.

His talent unfolded with plaster and clay.
He expressed himself with each figure he made.
Though he couldn't speak, he found a way,
The day he learned to paper Mache.

On Valentine's Day, he gave me a heart.
For every holiday, there was a different art.
Many of them hang on our living room wall.
The newer ones displayed in the hall.

I can remember the first time he went to camp.
I was extremely proud of my little champ.
Then I couldn't imagine that this day would come.
That the world would embrace all he has done.

# PERSISTENCE

Oh child, you got a whole lot of living to do.
Greater things in life are ahead of you.
When the voice of confusion tries to steer you wrong.
Know doing right not wrong gets you recognition.

You can know the joy of winning even after you lose.
Tho' there's pain in failing as you fall and you bruise.
There's one thing every winner should know.
Winning takes persistence.

Child, you got to have plans and you got to have aim.
Even if you don't earn money or fame.
Do whatever you do, as if you're getting paid,
Cause doing your very best is its own reward.

Don't let anybody think, you can't take the heat.
Don't allow them to take away your sweet.
Keep your glow going, because you got what it takes.
Don't ever give up or think that it's too late.

*(This is a song Lyric song can be found in the Songs by Ruth app)*

# VICES AND VIRTUE

Self-afflictions exist,
Hammer the frame of suffering,
Avoid the hands that render aid,
Attribute pain to others.

Selfishness resist,
Walk away from helplessness,
Gird its waist with desires,
Not compassion for others?

Greed consume others
Without regard for need,
Deprive victims,
As if untroubled by this.

But what compels generosity?
Does it take an avalanche?
Or the wind that blows leaves,
For a stranger to know her?

# CREATED HELL

If ten thousand angels
Failed to see my sorrow.

If my cries only echoed,

If God heard but refused me aid,
People did and acted the same,
Who could I trust or believe in?

If the burning in my chest were hell,
If there were error in my beliefs,
and expectations,

If I concentrated on those things,
Would I be comforted, rewarded,
Would grief miraculously be eradicated?

Due to those thoughts alone,
My troubles doubled.

# UNEXPLAINABLE!

Who chooses a frail person
For the most grueling tasks?

Person without awareness
To decipher mysteries,

Uneducated to document history,
Blind to envision beauty?

Helpless to be engaging,
Defenseless to overcome,

Stutterer to relay stories,
ordinary to be astonishing?

The God who defies logical thinking,
I believe, but no one can explain him.

# GONE!

My heart ached as his stopped.
As if he didn't know,
His loss would cause me sorrow.

Like rain melting drops of snow,
He slipped from me.

I will never forget his laughter,
Precious memory that remained
But gone is his presence.

He left; I wish to be carefree,
Not know the pain I feel.
For my troubles to be taken by the wind,
As though they never knew me.

There were no final goodbyes,
No complaint, not a hint,
Warning before he died.
Instead he passed on.

I sorrow alone,
Without understanding,
My many unanswered questions,
Life goes on without him.

# LIVING WITH ANGELS

As children, we used to run and play.
We stayed close until that tragic day.
What I was told didn't make sense.
They claimed that you killed yourself.

Now you are living with angels.
And our loss is heaven's gain.
You're free from troubles and pain.
Like we were when we were children.

I remembered when you were two.
You thought blinking lights laughed with you.
Then, you laughed back with them,
And laughed at the stories you'd tell.

In the military, you sky dived.
Had an aneurysm and survived.
So why did you take your life?
But this is what I tell myself.

Now you are living with angels.
And our loss is heaven's gain.
You're free from troubles and pain.
Like we were when we were children.

# SHOW ME HOW TO GROW

Wounded,
Defenseless,
Wallowing in my tears,
But no one cares.

Witnesses, I have none.
He has his reputation.
I carry the blame.

Weeping willow,
How do you grow?
When as far as weeping goes,
I am diminishing on the inside,
But I want to excel.

I can go on complaining,
Feeling like a victim,
I don't want to,
weeping willow, please,
just show me how to grow.

# SOUTH BOUND

I ran off at fifteen.
I had many painful days.
I wanted my dream life.
I hated the way I was raised.

I've learned a few things.
The street struggle is real,
And it wasn't where I should be.
Though my home was not ideal.

I'll take a South bound train;
And I'm headed back home.
I'm free from all my chains.
South bound to where I belong.

I was searching for affection.
Wish I could undo my actions.
I disrespected my parents.
I made some poor decisions.

I was forced to sell my body.
Many offered me drugs.
But no one truly loved me.
The streets were filled with thugs.

# FINALLY, HAPPY

I knew no gracious men
in the city of my torment.
They acted as if I didn't matter.
I tried to not focus on them but ahead.
My thoughts and memories were
of all I longed to accomplish.
Trampled on but determined,
I changed my location.
Return to the place that birth me.
Thrived where I was from, loved.
Rested untroubled, discovered,
supported where I wished to be,
finally relaxed and happy.

# COLOR ME! MAKE ME BRAND NEW.

Paint a magnificent Portrait.
Tells my unique story.

With every stroke
Illuminate my best features.

Highlight me superbly,
Capture my majestic character,
Simultaneously disperse my flaws.

Plaster me into a beautiful person.

Brilliantly clothe my contour
With gentleness, kindness, graciousness.

Cheerfully, tenderly and patiently
Drape me with compassion

That springs from the nurturing,
Caring, encouraging, supportive guidance,

Used to mold my beautifully created,
Inspirational life.

# LIFE'S NO GAME

Life's no game, but any can win.
It doesn't matter what the goal is.
Only that action navigates it.

If those who love you hold their applause,
And don't support your cause,
During the times, when that's a fact,
Focus on aim and not on that.

Success is not an alien to anyone,
But would remain a stranger
If one does not take the initiative to know her.

# VALUE!

Singular diamond,
Appraised, polished,
Sparkles unlike another.

Exists if uncut,
Unrecognized by others.

Valued not by authenticity,
Discovery, origination,
Or ownership, because it is.

Same is true of people,
Whether known or undiscovered,
Worth and beauty persists.

# REPLICATED DIFFERENCES

A single colored flower
Is different from its leaves.

Surrounding it variation,
different colors of relevance,
Adds beauty to flower beds.

Same plant produces disparity,
Acceptance without question
to reproduction.

So why can't we accept differences?
One ethnicity gave birth to others.

We are superior to plants
And all other mammals.

# OUT CRY!

For virgin ears
That haven't heard
words of love.

Hurt,
Sorry did not heal.

Confusion,
Explanation did not abate,

Know that you are loved.

May peace become your gift,
Joy your enabler,
Happiness your constant comforter.

Wear confidence as your strong suit.
In spite of situation, be thankful!

# HEALING TOUCH

Deprivation evokes sorrow,
more than cancer diagnosis,
High blood pressure, diabetes
weaken the body. Anguish

from abandonment cripples
the mind, steals joy,
Indifference is deadly.

Not only infants fail to thrive,
When left alone, untouched,
uncared for, so can anybody.

There is power in love,
Hope in compassion,
being comforted and cared for.

# COURAGE IN ILLNESS

The blues not the color or music,
Cold feet not from lack of courage,

Falling hair without chemotherapy,
Confusion, although not aged,
Accompanied my sickness.

Grasped differences between DCIS,
Type of non-invasive breast cancer,
And LCIS, an area of abnormal cell
in breast cancer diagnosis.

Wear a small scar on my chest,
Did not lose my breast.

Some days my weakened limbs
Become fatigued, still I walk with them.

Regain courage from smiling faces,
Blessed in my circumstances.

# TRADING PLACES

Fought illness like a lioness
Not wanting to be devoured,
Yet consumed by uncertainty.

Would I win or lose?
Shook my head at my biopsy result.

I trained for this,

Not to be battling illness,
To care for others, a nurse,

One who assist patients, to be empathetic,
Not to become disease's opponent.

In trading places,
I gained a different perspective,
Could identify, encourage others.

# I WEAR MY WOUNDS AS BADGES.

I beat my chest as if to say,
Captivity shaped me,
became my training arena,
and defiance's my coat of honor,

Inequality made me pliable,
Though that crushes people,
I'll never be trampled.

I regard pity as an enemy.
It strips people of dignity,
Adds insult to injury,

I beat my chest victoriously,
I wear my wounds as badges.

# THIS KIND OF LOVE

Love that cause hearts to flutter,
teenagers to giggle, knees to tremble,
Gives a natural high, many could do without
but want at their side.
They crave its intoxicating effects,
But none wants to pine or cry for love.
Desires it to be seen by friends and family,
Not shared, or filled by other people.

# THE LOVE I WANT IS
# THE LOVE I GIVE.

Or so I believed.
A love that's secure, free from fear,
for fear's torturous.

My love cherishes, is lovely,
More precious than jewelry,
Strengthens, is the best part of me,
a fountain of wellness, is glorious,
constant, doesn't create doubt,
or give cause to question devotion,
is unmovable, pleasant throughout
our moment together.

# NOT FOR MY EAR ONLY

I like my thoughts to be consistent.
Whether it is of love or brokenness.

I don't wish for my writings to be incomprehensible,
buried in complicated verbiage.

If I'm elated and love lifts me up,
My words reflect that.

If love tears me down, holds me back,
I can't speak to what I lack.

Loving is a good thing.
And grumbling isn't.
I express what I've been filled with.

I can't win if I'm defeated.
Can't shine if darkness embracing me.

So, keep shining sun, moon do your thing.
Clouds keep going by, don't linger.

Let the songs of my heart be heard,
treasured and not be for my ear only.

# RAIN

Rain, go somewhere else,
I'm pained within,
Wash away hurtful experiences.

Longed to hold onto innocence and beauty.
Clean injuries, redress and hide wounds,

Don't improve appearances, fix what's important.

Hearts need mending, attitudes need reconditioning,
But skin does not need fixing.

Difficulties comes down, intentionally to drown,
despite hurts, and efforts, life goes on.

# MIRROR, MIRROR, YOU THINK YOU KNOW ME,

Showing me like an icy lady.
That's not how I want to be seen.
Mirror, mirror, treat me like a queen.

Why don't you compliment my changes?
I'm becoming a lovely lady,
Show my good side sometimes,
I can be warm and friendly at times.

Mirror, Mirror, you think you know me,
Because of all you choose to see,
But you've lost your appeal,
Your reflections are unreal.

Images don't portray personality.
I loved and respected everyone around me,
Though at times I was harsh,
I wasn't as bad as I appeared to be.

Mirror, mirror, you need to see,
The fabulous that's inside me,
And admit that you didn't show,
All that others needed to know.

# CALCULATED RISK!

I've walked the streets of adversity.
Trampled upon by negativity,
I learned their language,
grind my teeth in fury.

Didn't allow any to persuade me,
clung to the dream I envisioned.
Romance desperation, befriended
Losers and winners the same.

Left ntozake shange choreopoem
On my desk for more than thirty years,
reminder of my aim and destination.

While trembling, I took risks,
Not fully knowing outcome,
But wanting freedom, my writings
To be known, trouble to resolve,
I chose to do, pursue all I wanted.

# QUIET DAY

For stillness:
Badgering to cease,
Troubled recovery,
attain peace, cries to desist,
Tranquility to wash
over all,

sounds of happiness
to assure, uplifting words
that adore,
The cruel to become calm,
simple strong,

For Sun rays to be tamed,
No more blisters or burns,
Struggles to not define
Capability of any mind,

For repulsiveness to fade,
Sounds of joy to be heard,
Celebration of a new world,
harm's defeat, a quiet day,
I wait.

# FROM MY WINDOW, I'VE BEEN WATCHING.

I saw the Boston marathon and nine-eleven.
Brave men jumped in without hesitation.
I felt the prayers that blanketed the heavens.

From my window, I saw children dying.
Their families become broken in sad times.
Such violence shouldn't keep reoccurring.
For killing is not a solution of any kind.

There's no tragedy on earth that I don't ever see.
That includes burning buildings and disease.
Wish I could stop the madness down below.
I miss the peace I used to see from my window.

From my window, I've reached out,
Trying to heal, bring unity to every man.
But they all need to stand hand in hand.
Forget differences and know that's my plan.

'N I promised I'll bless those who love others.
Not just relatives, but strangers as brothers.

# IN GOD, WE TRUST

There were ashes everywhere when the towers fell.
The images shown on television burnt in my head.
Once a vision of beauty, a mass grave they became.
I felt helpless and dropped to my knees and prayed.

God who would do this? I asked him then.
The shock, the confusion was wide spread.
Not just New York City, the entire world was on edge.

An act of terror sent dust as high as the heavens.
As if, God would hide His splendor from us.
When it is, He, America trusts
to comfort in tragic moments.

# TRIBUTE TO AMERICA AND PARIS

It's a great time to be alive,
Though many live with fear.

From the ashes, we'll rise.
Lather in the good that's here.

We'll build up, stand up,
Keep up and defy terror,

Until all realize violence is
A foolish way to be recognized.

Paris will continue to be,
A place lovers wish to be, dream

and walk together in love until
they reach great heights, like the Eiffel tower.

America also will flourish,
Remain free and strong
Because God is its foundation.

This land of peace is no one's enemy.
And is as its citizens believes,
A place where any can live, love and flourish.

# SIMPLY BEAUTIFUL

All have special qualities
Gifts that should be on display,
Hang on the wall of the hall of fame.

We are all beautiful in different ways.
Though some don't recognize it,
It's that way.

Children should to be taught,
beauty's unique as snowflakes,
and diverse as the universe.

Displayed in character or words,
turn heads, and warm hearts.
So, to be simply beautiful,
Our speech needs be graceful.

# TWEET FROM GOD

If you got a tweet from God what would you want it to say?
Come as you are; don't let anything stand in your way?
It doesn't matter what you wear or what's your address.
He's proud of you and loves you regardless.

If I got a tweet from God, I'd ask for forgiveness.
I'd want God to accept me as I am.
I wouldn't want to be turn away for being honest.
I'd want to know that He's proud of how I lived.

For him to see I'm no longer held captive.
I'd want him to not be ashamed of me,
But happy that I'm free and helped others to be.
I'd want him to understand I'm no longer chaotic.

If I got a tweet from God, I'd be ecstatic.
I would tell the world all about it.
We are all beautifully created and blessed.
'N I'd thank him for taking time to tweet to me.

# GOD LISTENS

I heard you claim to loved me,
And I feel the same.
'N I know you've been calling out.
There are many calling on my name.

Lift your brother up when he falls.
Do as though you're my helper.
You can assist others around.
Care brings the world together.

I feel let down many times.
When you think, I haven't answered.
Or doubted that I'm not there,
And my name gets unjustly slandered.

As the giver of peace,
I know love brings people
together, It doesn't beat up,
But assists, is kind to its neighbor.

# TO LOVE AND BE LOVED

I miss love in the day time.
I think about love at night,
Still, my fleeting heart never loved full-time.

Held hostage, afraid to love,
Conflicted, I couldn't reach-out.
I needed to be freed to be beloved.

My fear, I fear had me on the run.
It was easier,
To wrestle with a love that was done.

Yet, I burned and burned in flames of love,
Wishing to know what I don't.
I cried out to heaven above.

I stared at the flickering stars.
I watched floating clouds,
All done to squash my emotional war.

The fear, the fire consumed my soul,
As did my frolicking thoughts and desires.
Outwardly I was calm and in control,
For to love and be loved was still my goal.

# MY SUMMATION

Crushed by rejection, I was depressed.
I didn't volunteer to be a mess.
Was I curse or set apart? I fought
to end biasness, to be accepted,
Loved and not seen as a spectacle.

I unveiled myself because I no longer wish
to hide, be denied, for you to get to know me.

I prayed for delivery, still I wrestled,
Imprisoned by reality,
All unpleasantness I saw,
I felt persecuted but returned to where
I was: lenient, empathetic
to those who are where I stood,
rejected because of deficiencies,
being different but similar to all other beings.

# TO LIVE AS I IMAGINED.

I knew how to get what was mine in life.
And I'm not talking about birthright,
But all that was good, and I believed to be true.
Still I struggled, unsure of what I should do.

But I didn't want to be held back,
Because my hurt I couldn't forget.
I didn't want to be held back,
And live a life filled with regret.
I wanted to live as I imagined.

I believed the best is still to come.
And I've been holding on for some time now.
Others would have moved on.
But all my nights continue to turn to morn.

I couldn't openly live a lie.
Or claim to be happy when pained inside.
I chose to do what was right.
And didn't give up until I won the fight.

# IN THE ARMS OF GOD

I've asked, why me, many times.
I struggled most days with my troubles.
Though my mistakes were not crimes.
Life was never as easy as blowing bubbles.

But when I start to feel victimized,
I simply close my eyes.

I'm resting in the arms of God,
And I'm wanted and sheltered.
It's peaceful in the arms of God,
And that's all I need to remember.

I was broken and mistreated.
Excuses told me, no one was to blame.
But it made me feel defeated.
Although it didn't really put out my flame.

And there are daily reminders.
Things worth having doesn't come easy,
I don't need to wear blinders.
'Cause all that matters is the way love sees me.

# SONG OF THANKSGIVING.

It doesn't matter what I'm going through.
I'll always sing to you.
I'll lift my voice in praise.
You've honored me in many ways.

Once my faith was falling down.
I couldn't count on those around.
I got on my knees and prayed.
You helped me get through those days.

You're a God of second chances,
And you've caused me to see.
You gave me beauty from Ashes.
Thank you for loving me.

You've taken away my guilt and my shame.
I'll always bless your name.
I've no reason to cry,
Because you've given me wings to fly.

I've gone through many trials and I've grown.
I didn't do that on my own.
You were there leading me on.
My sadness and my fears are gone.

*(This is a song lyric in the songs by Ruth collection)*

# SWEET SPOT

I thought I lost my sweet spot.
I was wrestling with life a little bit.
I thought I lost my sweet spot,
I felt pushed far beyond my limits.

The hands of God were always there,
Even when I was drowning in despair.
The hands of God lead me to a place,
And it was there, that I was repaired.

It was as if he said, hello dear.
I don't want you to quit,
And don't take your eyes off me,
Not even for a minute.

I wanted a life without the scars.
So, I ignored his messages,
But in that moment, I was aware,
My sweet spot had reappeared.

*(This is a song lyric streaming in the Songs by Ruth app)*

# THE FINAL APPEAL

This is where we are now,
From here we can transform
put resources into resurrecting the wronged.

To step up, move forward,
seeing eyes has to speak out.
To upgrade our standard
and not remain fixed
Or stagnant,

We should hold hands.
See others as human,
a fellow man,
souls originating from
the same source.
Differences merely perspective
And or conditioning.

# THANK YOU FOR
# READING MY BOOK

The End